Ring of Fire

LISA JARNOT was born in Buffalo, New York in 1967. She is the author of several chapbooks as well as a full-length collection of poems, *Some Other Kind of Mission*, (Burning Deck Press, 1996). She currently lives in New York City and is completing a biography of the American poet Robert Duncan which will be published by the University of California Press in 2005.

Ring of Fire

LISA JARNOT

SALT

PUBLISHED BY SALT PUBLISHING
PO Box 937, Great Wilbraham PDO, Cambridge CB1 5JX United Kingdom
PO Box 202, Applecross, Western Australia 6153

First published by Zoland Books, Boston USA 2001
Second enlarged edition 2003

Printed and bound in the United Kingdom by Lightning Source

Typeset in Swift 9.5 / 13

ISBN 1 84471 007 6 paperback

SP

1 3 5 7 9 8 6 4 2

for Elizabeth Willis

Contents

Acknowledgments

Some of the poems included in this volume were originally published in the following magazines, chapbooks, and books:

Bombay Gin, The Colorado Review, Compound Eye, Downtown Brooklyn, Facture, Gare Du Nord, Gas: High Octane Poetry, Grand Street, The Hat, The Impercipient, Jacket, Kenning, Lingo, Mass Ave, Mike and Dale's Younger Poets, Object, The Portable Boog Reader, Shiny, Stand, Talisman, The Transcendental Friend, Verse, Washington Review, The World, and *Zazil.*

The Eightfold Path (a+bend press, San Francisco), *Heliopolis* (rem press, Cambridge), *new mannerist tricycle* (Beautiful Swimmer Press, Brooklyn), *Sea Lyrics* (Situations Press, New York), and *Two of Everything* (Meow Press, San Diego).

Ring of Fire (Zoland Books, Boston).

Odi et amo. quare id faciam, fortasse requiris.
nescio, sed fieri sentio et excrucior.
—CATULLUS

I. The Book of Providence

The Bridge

That there are things that can never be the same about
my face, the houses, or the sand, that I was born under the
sign of the sheep, that like Abraham Lincoln I am serious
but also lacking in courage,

That from this yard I have been composing a great speech,
that I write about myself, that it's good to be a poet, that I look
like the drawing of a house that was pencilled by a child,
that curiously, I miss him and my mind is not upon the Pleaides,
that I love the ocean and its foam against the sky,

That I am sneezing like a lion in this garden that he knows
the lilies of his Nile, distant image, breakfast, a flock of birds
and sparrows from the sky,

That I am not the husband of Cassiopeia, that I am not
the southern fish, that I am not the last poet of civilization,
that if I want to go out for a walk and then to find myself
beneath a bank of trees, weary, that this is the life that I had,

That curiously I miss the sound of the rain pounding
on the roof and also all of Oakland, that I miss the sounds of
sparrows dropping from the sky, that there are sparks behind
my eyes, on the radio, and the distant sound of sand blasters,
and breakfast, and every second of it, geometric, smoke
from the chimney of the trees where I was small,

That in January, I met him in a bar, we went
home together, there was a lemon tree in the back yard,
and a coffee house where we stood outside and kissed,

That I have never been there, curiously, and that it never was
the same, the whole of the island, or the paintings of the stars,
fatherly, tied to sparrows as they drop down from the sky,

O rattling frame where I am, I am where there are still
these assignments in the night, to remember the texture
of the leaves on the locust trees in August, under the
moonlight, rounded, through a window in the hills,

That if I stay beneath the pole star in this harmony of
crickets that will sing, the bird sound on the screen,
the wide eyes of the owl form of him still in the dark,
blue, green, with shards of the Pacific,

That I do not know the dreams from which I have come,
sent into the world without the blessing of a kiss, behind the
willow trees, beside the darkened pansies on the deck beside
the ships, rocking, I have written this, across the back of the
sky, wearing a small and yellow shirt, near the reptile house,
mammalian, no bigger than the herd,

That I wrote the history of the war waged between the
Peloponnesians and the south, that I like to run through
shopping malls, that I've also learned to draw, having been
driven here, like the rain is driven into things, into the
ground, beside the broken barns, by the railroad tracks,
beside the sea, I, Thucydides, having written this, having
grown up near the ocean.

Dictionary

As a small south american squirrel
inhabiting mostly mountainous regions
would feed on lizards half-way between
poles of the tropics, I too would fall
heartbreaked in the settlement of feuds
or the fields of kentucky.

When the moss grows high between the
perennials and disordered mimmocks weep,
these dainty fastidious gestating mammals
break for leavened bread and sup between
the rows of trees, lifting like friars
some heavy books in sunlight's morning
windows where the mollusks row in scion's
quadragesimal phyla.

Tell Me Poem

Tell me why you don't
want to know about the
snake cults in ancient
greece and then tell me
why someone started all
the tin foil on fire on
avenue b and then tell
me the story about osgood
and ferocious the giant
squirrels.

Ode

For let me consider him who pretends to
be the pizza delivery man and is instead
the perfect part of day, for the fact he is a
medium, for the eight to twelve inches
of snow he tends to be, for he who covers
the waterfront, for he that was hand-
made in a tiny village in japan, for
that he is more than just an envelope
or inside-out balloon, for that he can
always find the scotch tape, for that
he resembles a river in mid-December
muddied over, for that he has seen the
taxi cabs on fire in the rain, for that he is
like the heat beneath the desk lamp, for
that he is not a tiny teal iguana, for that
it is he who waits for me inside cafes, for
that he has hands and legs, for that he
exceeds the vegetable, for that he is the
rest of the balance continuing huge.

Brooklyn Anchorage

and at noon I will fall in love
and nothing will have meaning
except for the brownness of
the sky, and tradition, and water
and in the water off the railway
in New Haven all the lights
go on across the sun, and for
millennia those who kiss fall into
hospitals, riding trains, wearing
black shoes, pursued by those
they love, the Chinese in the armies
with the shiny sound of Johnny Cash,
and in my plan to be myself
I became someone else with
soft lips and a secret life,
and I left, from an airport,
in tradition of the water
on the plains, until the train
started moving and yesterday
it seemed true that suddenly
inside of the newspaper
there was a powerline and
my heart stopped, and everything
leaned down from the sky to kill me
and now the cattails sing.

What In Fire Did I, Firelover, Starter of Fires, Love?

The glow of it in early winter, the barn that Eric Bartlett
and Ronnie Burke burned down on Sturgeon Point Road
in 1981 and not on purpose, the coils of voluminous
smoking snake pellets set off in the driveway and on the
porch steps with the neighbors kids, the activity of Jim in
finding the biggest log outside the house to put into the
fire, the burning things upon the beach—paper cups, straws,
tires, and also driftwood, the building of all such things to a
cone of six feet high on or near the night of the fourth of july,
annually, the specific red candle flame in the kitchen at
two a.m. in 1987 having consumed a mushroom stem
and cap and after having returned from the supermarket
neon, the silver lighter Peter gave me in 1991 that I
subsequently lost when I lived in the back room off the
kitchen in a house on Ashland Avenue, the napalm that
we made with styrofoam and gasoline and flung from slingshots
onto moving cars while burning, the brownish edge of plant
leaves in the middle of the living room beneath the skylight,
equidistance between the two giant fish tanks in the place
in Oakland by the phone without an ashtray, the bucket thing
of ashes outside Kevin's bedroom window, the clicker for
the gas stove with the broken hook that couldn't hang upon
the wall, its reflectiveness in midday so as to be nearly
invisible, the imagined heat of the outer planets and all burning
that there is, the oppositeness of it to appliances known as
fridge, the barbecue we never had in Brooklyn cuz the charcoal
was no good, the comet that we saw from the same porch
with the barbecue which was a fire in the sky, the supposed
end of the world, the subterranean lakes of fire, the song called
ring of fire, the words firecracker, firedog, and firehose, the fire
in the fennel stalk and also then Prometheus, all general ideas
of warmth and glowingness, the variety of foods that can be

cooked with it, the use of it to see when there's no electricity,
its ability to melt wax, the way it starts from broken glass
reflections, the way it melts sand into useful glass,
the way it can be used to shape things into glass-shaped
swans and also other birds.

Found Text

The deer mistook their reflections for deer
and the deer mistook their reflections for
other deer and the deer apparently
mistook their reflections for sheep and
what the deer mistook their reflections for
isn't certain and the deer were removed
from the scene, being deer, before being
removed and mistaking reflections of the
other deer for the sheep the deer were
removed and the deer deciding to join
them joined the deer having mistaken
reflections of sheep for the deer in the
plate glass windows.

Autobiography

I didn't sleep with anyone for six months until I met X. While I was sleeping with Y I also slept with Y's girlfriend. While I was sleeping with Y's girlfriend I also slept with S and T. During the six months between sleeping with Y and sleeping with X I spent a lot of time with K. I never slept with K but J slept with K and Y's girlfriend and also with S. After leaving Y and before meeting X I didn't sleep with anyone for six months.

Anomalous circus events take the shape of mandible density in the great outer planets. Newly created seafloors at the ridges of divergent plate boundaries and adjacent plates are moved apart to make room for divergent plate glass boundaries in the seafloor at the ridges of the seafloor. When I was twelve I made out with my cousin on the 4th of July. At the ridges of the seafloor and adjacent plates are seafloor fauna moved apart on seafloors for the plates of glass divided by adjacent plates of seafloors moved apart.

One Saturday in July the cable man came to the door and she let him in. Once he was standing on the edge of the balcony and he saw a dog-headed man on the beach. Every Wednesday the phone rang and someone named Vegas left a message for someone named Cynthia about the cast parties as the Python Club. It was that simple but somehow it seemed all wrong.

Still Life

Where we finally move closer, but instead we don't move closer at all, we just have an understanding that we want to move closer, which is a form of moving closer, or at least something to think about, that it was an idea, moving closer, though not ultimately satisfying, though something, on one or two or three occasions, during a single night, moving closer, and the sands accumulate into sand paintings, that are colorblind, and filled with raccoons, and the steps of the sand toward the pyramid of sand are altered, wearing pumpkins on their heads, wishing to be loved, in the steps of the sand, terrified, or not terrified, moving closer, identifying with raccoons, on certain evenings, that maybe to go from there, because obviously, the sand and raccoons accumulate, taking years, listening to the traffic, saying is it quiet where you live, near the sand and the raccoons, in a quiet room, near the sounds of all the traffic that moves closer, on the periphery, that the thing is this, accumulating, getting closer, to the raccoons and the traffic that moves closer, having moved, having said that moving closer is ideal, having said thank you, and so forth, that the so forth is moving closer, forward, toward what in most of the universe would have been a scene, where the sand is forgotten, and the raccoons, and the accumulation of pyramids, and clothing items, and various identifications, and so forth, but instead, one by one, or one, or two or three times awkwardly, there is news, and there are raccoons, and the raccoons are screeching in the yard, as if to say something about the grains of sand, at opposite sides of the universe, screeching, with their suits and ties, bringing news, like Tom Brokaw, colorblind, reliable, and standing in the sand, and the news, which should not be true, but is, that there are raccoons, screeching, outside, in the traffic, near the sand, and on the news, and the curious figure that is him, there, who is reliable, and like the sand, accumulating, rightly, while how wrong it is, the news, that there is a rightness about him, the news of the raccoons, so close enough, and safely in the sand.

Valley of the Shadow of the Dogs

He could be so far outside himself, generating body heat, far from the telephone, in a room, heated, with the outside of his thoughts, turning, with precision, for the reasons he would know, nearer to god and the mountains and the outside of the room, with the chairs, perceived as objects, always slightly passed, looming, on the forefront, like cake, looming, on the forefront, ambitious, like a sumac leaf, lovely, a wing, with wings and made of cake, having counted let me count, one, the ways that there are, unused, potentially useful, held at a distance like a flower filled with tiny bugs, loved and lovely, without raccoons, beside the spiders, smashed on the sides of the forks, lovely the form in the meadow of the shadows of the dogs, howling, reckless, unusual, unfulfilled, with the christmas lights, steady, and how close I am to myself, and how close they are to the sumac leaves, lovely, against the rain, falling out, fully heated, from the inside of his head, with spiders, in a meeting, against the rain, given to this disposition, equally talented, talkative, talking in tongues, beyond the heads of the cows, friendly, on the staircase, friendly, where I waited and the city moved, drenched beneath the sumac leaves, having fallen, into the field, where the dogs are, looming, in the forefront, in the shadow of the gods, dreaming of being alone, relieved, heated, steady on the trees beside their wings, riding on the backs of all the bears, and the bears, relieved to be the sumac leaves, and the sumac leaves, relieved to be the bears, and the spider, on the plate, relieved to be just so, wanting to be loved, where the city moved, and then I moved, and the pins all moved, out of place, tetanus-like, having syllables, wishing to love, wishing to love the ocean and the ski runs and the sand, wishing to love the sheep, converging, on the frontispiece, having thrown the ball, equally having thrown the ball and having thrown it, into the leaves, near the trees and all the dogs, meditating, on the coffee cups, meditating, on the backs of all the bears.

The New Life

I eat steak and live on the big neon avenue and fear strangers,
admire my neighbors, the drug store, and the bus,

I as an addict live addicted to the avenue, in the dark folds
late at night, addicted to sleep and lavender,

I went into the liquor store to buy a bottle of wine,
loving you and the liquor store, the lavender bottles, the
many directions in which the hairs on my lover's head
fall at twilight reading Roland Barthes,

I went into the sidewalk to reconstruct the broken glass,
loving sleeping I went into dark folds late at night
loving my lover but also addicted to fearing and loving
my neighbor and the types of wine,

I crawled in through the window and loving my neighbor
I loved my lover and counted the hairs on his head,

I as an addict am an addict and the street below is below
and my lover has countless hairs on his head and the poise
of living on the big neon avenue where I cut myself and
cooked the dark steak, emerging from the folds of lavender,

I cut myself and then my lover cut himself, and someone
puked on the side of a van

I fear the fears my lover fears and fearing strangers fear
the steak and twilight reading Barthes

I love him steadily reading fears and quiet the twilight reading
and quiet my lover and quiet my fears, admiring lovers
and fearing handsome strangers in the drug stores
near the puked on van,

I run toward him in a bus in a dream, my lover puked on by the
children on the bus,

Coveting the drug store hip-hop lavender flowers, never quite
understanding what's been said, I admire cutting my steak,
the street below is filled with all the neighbors' heads and lovers
close behind the window weightless eating steak

I read the newspapers about the avenues and my lavender
photographed next to the wine,

I think my lover will be photographed and I am concerned about
the avenue itself, assuming neon characteristics, sometimes
casting shade,

I shade my eyes from the avenue where my lover and I make
love and the neighbors love their neighbors and the neon
characteristics of nightclubs shade the photo's eye, expecting
too much of the avenue like an unfinished painting
contrasting churches and contrasting love

I walk backward toward the street and love to be so backward
and love the lover's neighbor and casting shadows backward cast
the wine and types of love,

I close slowly avenues of poise assuming love and folds of
lover's hair,

I close slowly the sidewalk to find the broken glass, going toward
my lover to find the folds of likeness in the mirror made of glass
and waiting slowly close,

And loving how we meant to be sleeping I love the avenue
where we sleep and love the neighbors, vigilant, never quite
asleep, near the sides of vans,

I, slowly, closed with lavender, wake the lover waiting on the
avenue of glass.

The Age of the Velocipede

You are not a wounded animal, animal, you are not the voice of
god, you are not a bright and shiny terradactyl in the hot
museum night, you are not the person who can learn to speak in
french, you are not the traffic as it all moves down on 12th Street,
you are not the tar today on cab wheels as they move down in the
street, you are not the specks of glass inside the tar beneath the
wheels on 12th Street in the street, you are not the springtime or
the winter or the most autumnal rain, you are not the cars that
catch on fire in the sidestreet near the projects near con ed, you
are not the con ed man who came when I was naked, you are not
the terrier who walks between the pigeons in the park, you are
not the slice of upturned pizza on the sidewalk in the rain, you
are not the guy who sells the cigarettes for quarters in the
newstand in the rain, the guy who drives the cabs out in the tar
out in the rain, the guy who works inside of the bodegas in the
rain, you are not the snowstorm that we had at noon, the
wounded snow, or taxicab, or rain, you, animal, look at the
animal that you are, wounded, and then walking in short dactyls
like the upturned pizza in the park, the friendly cablike animal
that crosses against traffic in your rollerblades, you are the
animal looking for no one, you are the one who is inside all of
the soup, you are the one in the tar heaps and soup cans and
porches on 12th street on days when it rains, you are the one who
goes by your name in the book with the names in the books in
the rain, you are the dreams of the cashiers who face this rejec-
tion and ice cream and pies, you, wounded animal, slicing pieces
edgewise of yourself and off your skin, swimming in the small
ponds and the pools, the terminals abound, the onramps over-
shadow you, with theatres and movie screens, and movie stars
and pies, you with the ice cream and you with the popcorn and
you with the pies, you who have dreamt that you've killed dennis
hopper, eating popcorn, watching marlon brando on t.v., you,
infinitely influenced, you, stuck in awe of superstores on many
city blocks, you of the late night reflections of neon, you of the
vastest and massivest parks, animal like, walking through times

square, wounded, animal like animal, the hippopotamus and chicken that you are, the person who resembles all the ocelots in zoos, the monkey and the polar bear in midtown in the circus in the rain, so far from all sea coasts, so far from highways with the trucks in which you did arrive, you the animal, the not not animal, you the animal you are, in a crowded theatre where you wait for love and love waits for you, where the dactyls small and fuzzy walk across the park and call your name from rollerblades and skates, you animal, you are the animal walking upon the tepid sidestreet, you are the animal wolf and the head of the animal nobody knows what's its name, you are the giant tree sloth inside of the stained glass and next to the sun, you are the one in the hot tub, the sauna, and steam room where strangers get mugged, you are the one of the animals waiting in lines, at bus stops, at malls, in the rain, you of the libraries stalking of books, you of the beach and amusements and rides, you, animal, wounded as the animal you are, you are not a pencil or a deer-skin or the rain, you are not the god that is a pencil in the rain, you are not a deerskin or a library or mall, you, animal, slightly wounded, slightly blue, and like the neon in the blue and wounded rain, you are not the one who knows about philosophy or ezra pound, you are not the lightning streaks or airplanes in the tiny distant sky, you are not the deerskins in the high and distant mountains of the holy land of cabs, you are this animal, you are the animal you are and you know how to be, you are not the secret garbage man who takes my garbage when I put it on the porch, you are not a porch and you are not a person with a porch and you are not protracted like a porch out in the rain, you are not the thing that writes about the things that I am not, you are not the sun, and you are not a radio, and you are not a garage sale, a lawn sale, a circus, swap meet, or the rain, you have never been to swap meets but you have been to the zoo, you have not been tranquilized or showed up on a golf course or from inside of a big tin, and you are not the shoe polish, and you are not the type of thing that comes inside of cans, and you are not some

tiny mints, and you are not the chickens or the deer, and you
don't live inside the oppenheimer zoo, and you are not a flying
bird or snail, and you are not an abductee, and you are not the
one who goes there where a third goes by you too, you are
unidentifiable inside the dark of night, you of the farm land, you
of the winter, the windmills, the ice cream, the porch and of
rome, you of the coffee and cigarettes telephone book and the
rain, you are you, the comet shooting through the sky, the arc of
the moon that you are as you lie in reflections on windshields in
rain, you are the eyeballs of deers in the headlights of cars and
the trucks in the rain, you are the one who was born by the river,
you were born by the river in a little tent, you were born by the
river in a little tent near the terrible patagonians, you are not the
patagonians, and you have no tent, and there is no river, and you,
in the summer, in front of the fan, turned on, taking long and
ancient unexplained vacations, you, on the bus, on the street, in
the rain, rain on animal, wounded in the snow, rain on with the
porch lights, ice cream and the rain, you, animal, wounded in
bordellos in the rain, looking at the sky from down inside the wet
suits where you are, for you the shark and surfer too, the builders
of the men, you, automaton, destroyer of cities and ships, clinging to the downside of a monkey, you are not a lupine, lupine,
you are an animal, awake inside the bee hive state, you are what
the moon has been, awake and somewhat animal in rain, on the
roof in the screen in the theatre inside the tar beside the cab
wheels on the street and through the window in the rain, go on,
you animal, complete in all your excess animalness that you are,
you are not the animal that licks the fuzz from off the tops of
blankets, you are not the howling noise from four flights down
on ludlow street in spring, you are not the broken books, the
broken screen, the broken leaking toilet, go on animal, tar base
for the cabs and tar and sidestreets in the rain, go on you animal
of stick ball and libraries and rain, go on to be the animal you
are, unextinct and glowing in the moonlight in the depths you
have that hide inside this most autumnal rain.

II. Sea Lyrics

*Callifornia, a large country of the West Indies, lying between 116°
and 138° W. long. and between 23° and 46° N. lat. It is uncertain
whether it be a peninsula or an island.*
—ENCYCLOPEDIA BRITANNICA, 1768.

I am a partially submerged boat on the waterfront of Jack London Square on a Sunday morning buying jam. I am flesh-colored and pale, in an indian head dress cracking chestnuts and eating roots, in the fissure between the bus lines, with the smell of burnt toast in the can-crushing lot, in the inside-out tomato yards, where I am riding all the bicycles through tunnels to the lawn, where I am on a downtown bus, partially submerged, I am krill and various large birds, the color grey of the sidewalk, a small opossum, in the breaking glass in isolation in the sun, I am waiting for the swamps and smoke of eucalyptus in the breeze, I am stuck in traffic near the mudflats on the bay, I am aimless and have several new tattoos.

Today I am rivets of sails in a log cabin where Jack
London lived in Alaska until they moved his cabin here
where we collect the change to buy our drinks and eat
the free hors d'oeuvres, where the neighbors are
somewhat pleased beside the railroad trains, where the
vague sense of the Union Pacific is with opossums of
freeways and you, where we've assembled plastic birds all
morning, where the airplanes fill the plastic sky, where
the fish are brightly colored on the lawn, where an
underwater bird is pummeled on the sidestreet, where we
take hallucinogens and wander through museums, where
the people construct the artificial ponds, where
theosophists arrive on all the hillsides, where I have
been bowling all morning, where we have been airplanes
and also the plastic small birds, where this is the type of
leisure that I am, where these are the largest of fires,
where the highway trembles on the edge of the
waterfront square.

I am collecting ceramic dogs and cats, I am awake early today to go to the lawn from the shower to the vacantest lot with all the pit bulls and the cars, I am waiting for the man to come in through the window, I am sitting on the roof devoured by the smog, I am directing you to a sushi bar, I am cooking only foods with milk and eggs, I am a tiny frozen squid.

I am here inside the freezer where you left me, I am
the unobstructed silence of the avocado dawn, I am the
neighborhood of foreign things, I am the telemarketer
of evening, I have only donuts and the doors are locked,
I am as thick as the morning down on Broadway, I am
walking near the freeway as it shakes, I am the overpass
and shattered in the midst of day, I am the last of the
partially submerged vehicles on the waterfront on
Sunday buying jam.

I am the waterfront and I cover the waterfront and all
the boats all know me, I am the foreignest of birds and
the shadows of sails upon martinis, I am underwater
buying jam and drinking stolen coffee, I am pelagic now
and sober, having recently discovered all the birds.

I am not quite yet the harmony of spheres, I have been hunting prey and building bridges for several years now on and off, I am the foam of obstruction in the foam of obstruction I am, I am the open bridge, I am the falling away from a baseball game across the earth on the edge of the islands and jail.

I have come from here to there on multi-colored
subways through the multi-colored lawns with wet feet
being webbed and nearly sober where the baseball teams
are frenzied and Peralta herds his cows, where abutting
all the artificialist lagoons are moonlight and the sound
of wheels, where the palm trees are imagined, where the
knotted branches ring the edge of all the hillsides by the
park, where in the lunar tides I fall outside the porch
into tequila, I am at the library with the health food
stores, I am upon the roof to glare across the city where
I am, I am trembling like the traffic, I am on the backs
of motorcycles in the pull of tides in astrology and far
from Detroit.

I sell real hair at the real hair sale near the shrimp boats
on the pier, where there are no crickets where there is no
weather where there are no squirrels where there are
some bison, where the wax museum dummies and the
Tony Bennett man are singing Chances Are, where there
are inside the Shakespeare Gardens rows of roses and a
tiny stream, where I'm waiting by the stage door with the
stop watch man, where I lie in boxes filled with ice and
all the pony fish and prawns, where I am leaving here on
Thursday, where I am at a pancake house to say goodbye,
where I am studying pianos, where from from where the
pizza is so seldom good, from the rows of coconuts in
cans, from all the ancient chocolates, from the lack of
all mayonnaise, from how lost I am and strange to all
the underwater birds, from in the park with railroad cars
and one pagoda, from the cranes and pulleys littering
the estuary even in late May.

We have been eating toast all morning, no longer worried about who we might offend, in a noon-day riot of the mandarins in church, with several chiropractors in the dusk where vertigo rolls past the fog and the fog rolls past the water's edge and the water rolls down hillsides.

I am barbecuing eucalyptus pigs of hills and brightly colored housetops, I am waiting for my senses to come back, I am a cabbalistic moment all in black, I am your drunken Irish brother and the plantains on the lawn, I am the tourists hording sharks teeth, I am the empty grain silos of Bernal Heights and god, and I am you on the back of a motorcycle crossing Dolores in the pineapple groves of Elvis Costello, sleeping all night, inside of the artificialist lagoons, beyond the palm trees, I am a drag queen named Heather not quite ready for New York.

I am loving you beside the man with his pants down on the highway where you are love itself and dying, and from the inside of the train the subway tracks are dangerous, I am dangerous and undangerous also and a big shopping store I am, I am for the hillsides bowling, I am unlike all the other counties in this wood, I am clipped by cars while crossing major streets, I am forced to wake at dawn and go to work with all the pitbulls, cans, and coffee crushing lots, I am the tiny specks of detritus and metal that flake in the streets, I am the stray opossum at the undersides of highways, I am the screaming man at midnight in the lot.

As a community service offering I am stuffing envelopes
and studying the ties, I am here with the opossums near
the waterfront, I am wandering unhindered by the food
chain, I am fond of the can crushing lot and ride my
bike around it, I am at a sidestreet fair still looking for
Der Wienerschnitzel, I am all tattoos and deejays, I am
in love with the parking lot, I am trying on new shoes, I
am with these murals of the cows in towns near towns
and bridges.

I won't go to the waterfront anymore, I am basking on a
beach far from the army, I am pointing to a thousand
speckled birds, I am watching the salads roll down to the
shore, I am on the grounds of Mission High School with
the murderers, I am near the edge of all the bungalows, I
am reaching toward the pineapples to reach, I am
dreaming the dreams I hardly know and know I have
tattoos, I am in the ambulance at dawn, I am in this
town beneath where you have jumped from bridges row
by row, from the midtown light, I am in the dreams
Lucretius, I have helped you to assemble all the
mammals on the lawn.

Both sea lions and sea leopards cough in the halls of our sleep while we play pinball, I am ebbing in and out, I am dreaming dreams I hardly know and have tattoos, I am dreaming dreams outside of dreams and fish tanks and the spanishest of music.

In these tenements, inside this subterranean roadway, upon this stream gone underground, from the top of the hill and the door of the shoe store mid-town, I am dreaming dreams I hardly know are dreams and in the causeway, I am standing under the cracked bannister observing all the parts, I am a subterranean cave dweller clubbing fish, I have seen the light of day with all the roaches, I have hardly noticed all the artificialist lagoons.

And I am so said amazons, Lucretius, I am clinging to
the baked goods and the liquor store, I am nearly
spanish and then nearly other things, I am cutting you
with broken glass, I am a tiny frozen squid, I am in
tenements with amazons who dream of me and
plantains.

I am standing on the corner where Huey Newton got shot
but you thought that he was Huey Lewis.

I have been a long time upon this bridge wearing the inestimable freedom of the dawn, a new tattoo, in the dust upon the window in the tiny rain of fields, in the north to point at flocks and speckled birds, in the dark to grasp at windhovers, to hawks and also habitrails, to the third rail to the watching you, I am trying to be calm and listen for instructions, having crossed the bridge in all the cars, I am and the earth is on edge, I am the speed we are at when we are underground.

And especially from hot tubs at the parties with the small ceramic cows and brie, astral-projecting, and next to all comedians, from inside the t.v.s, to the most exciting ocean, inside the several redwoods, across the sparrows nesting in the porchlights on the porch.

Where the mailman comes to, and so to the bridges and tattoos I am, an albatross in the hottubs of dawn, and so to the living room parents, and so to the amazons who call me Lucretius.

I have been a long time in this story on the bridge inside
tattoos and wearing avocados, and I can think only of
myself, and I can steal the books in bookstores, and I
can collect cans at all the can and crushing lots, and I
am here to wait in line with others near the lawns, and I
am being shot at on the sidestreet, and I am hording all
the plastic pigs, and I am practicing with others for the
dawn, from rooftops where the hills are all on fire with
the most usual of circumstances, where the fish are kept
in large tanks and a black smoke settles on the roof,
where the neighbors harbor pitbulls between the cars,
where the strange small apples bounce across the tar
upon the roof, where opossums cross against the flow of
traffic, where the streetlights blink and flicker on, where
the plastic and the airplanes fill the sky, where we live
beside the most chinese of oceans, where I gamble in the
empty and where winterless I am.

And I have been a long time in this story of the
avocados of the dawn, and I have been a long time in
this story on the bridge, and I have been a long time on
this bridge, and I have listened to the overpass at dawn
with plastic mammals, and it is early evening, and I
invent a fish named Fred, and we have found the
avocados, and I am in the amazon of dreams, and I have
dreamt of tattoos in the plastic windows, and I am in the
rainy season near the lawn.

At dawn bent at odd angles the exercisers in the yard
speaking only dialects of fog, there were fish and then
tattoos, where we walked upon the waterfront of cave
bluffs, where the waterfront held shrimp, where there
were three dozen tourists behind the Thailand disco
beat, where the ferry left at dawn, where the buses never
came, where the sidewalk was all buckled, where the
customs seemed all strange, where I walked in shadows
of the eucalyptus night, where I seldom rode in cabs,
where I never owned a blue and shiny truck, where you
slowly bobbed your tea bag, where the apple trees turned
black, where I washed the fish inside the fountain in the
park, where I had been a long time in this story on the
bridge, where I have been wearing avocados all day,
where I am all tattoos and dreams of fashion, across the
glare of the roof, near the church of Thelonius Monk,
where I have seen the soot upon the windows of tattoos.

This is a jumbo prawn and these are all the mudskippers
inside of rusted cans, these are the circles underground
revolving with the habitrails of squirrels, this is a
dangerous underground stream from which we grow
the underground tomatoes, these are the tattoos of dawn,
this is the tiny metal hatchet near the bed, this is the
sound of my television, that is the sound of the tunnels
of the highway.

Massive and damp, on the ell curve by the Cliff House,
next to the nude beach on the barrios that point, where I
used to like the Grateful Dead but now I'm just a
satanist, this is the Cafe Boheme where I spend my time,
these are the sneakers I'd like to look cool in, this is the
hallway with plantains and people I know, these are my
neighbors, that is the jukebox place, these are the people
who sleep on my steps, this is the man in the
laundromat who wishes he was Carol Burnett.

I am bludgeoned by this most exotic ocean, currently, I
am in the post office with the prison cells and tides, I
am with the fires in the eucalyptus fog, I am clearing
and the colors are all changing, I am changing colors in
the lift of fog, I am almost to Japan, I am circles and the
squirrels revolve, I am missing plastic pets, I am
predictions of the sounds of tides and this.

I am this Santa Ana wind and we are bowlers, we are at
the haircut man, I have divulged so little of the avocado
dawn, I am waiting to buy coffee near the docks upon
the square, I am all the hot dogs and the roof of city
hall, I am hardly standing in the kamikaze rain, I am of
the new year sober now, I am inside of all the
horoscopes at once, I am the rainy part of early fall
expecting to go back across the bridges, I am near the
greenish plantains down the street, I am the subtler
angles of the sunlight from the surface of the moon, I
am here to yet predict the dawn, I am getting better like
the oceans on the sidestreet, I am surrounded by water, I
am walking sideways near the church in Watsonville
upon the orange line at Lammas Tide.

This is from which I came expecting to see others, for
the others from which they came and came I in the
generations fog, from the fog of fog's tattoos, from the
avocado sunlight, from the avocados and the fog to
where I came, this is from where I came and to which I
came and from what I came down to the library, this is
from which then came the plantains of the dawn and all
graffiti, I came this way and this is from which I came,
and from the sun and from inside the tiny plastic
mammals, from this palisade and from this palisade,
from the advent of street preachers on this block, from
the church on the corner where I walk again and
sideways, from the countless vacant lots all filled with
eucalyptus trees, from this part of the walk and at this
angle, and from this stout and from the top of this most
certain hill, beside along and down into our sleep, in
these halls and only to our dreams, from the surf upon
the Cliff House, down the surge of waterways in dark, of
each condition from which I came to come from with
the avocado dawn, where I am looking for Japan, where
I expect the palisades to fall, from inside of this
Atlantis, from where we rise like science, from where I
walk down sidestreets with a gun.

From the telemarketers of dawn to the wheatgrass
South of Market, in the sidestreet eating mushrooms
holding guns, for the greyish colored hills so patient
in the morning, for the stifling avocados of the
subterraneanmost fish stores, for the shark's teeth on
the shore, for all half-eaten surfers, for the pier with all
the sink holes on the edge, for the most misplaced of
onramps, for the holding cells and gambling rooms of
dusk upon the fog.

I am holding the guns in the attics of downtown stores
and sewing buttons on the Neiman Marcus pants suits, I
am in the breakroom holding coffee with my gun, I am
asking you to help me, I am at the ocean from the tops of
towers with the murals of the cows and factory workers
paid for by the Coits, I am watching all the tiny lights on
all the hills go on and off in darkness, I am waiting for
catastrophes inside t.v.s, I am jumping from the bridges
tempted by the waters far beneath, I am on the edge of
Lucretius where Peralta brought his cows to play pianos,
I am travelling by bus and I am travelling by horseback, I
am not sure where I am and I am travelling to edges made
of night, I am not sure where I am and I am travelling to
edges made of rock in avocado night, I am travelling to
the edges to the plane to where I am to cross the parking
lot to stand upon the median to edges made of rock in
avocado night.

III. Dumb Duke Death

Dumb Duke Death

down dire
death day
dim dale
ding dong

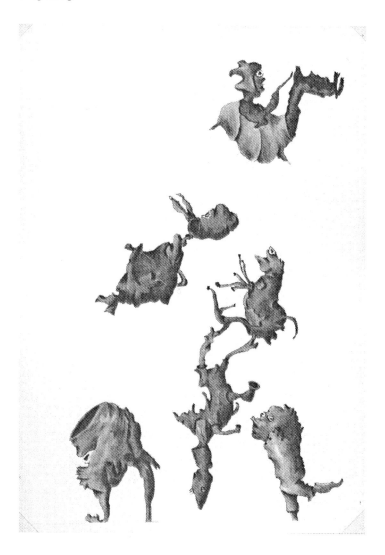

dip down
dame chase
cheap date
dance dodge

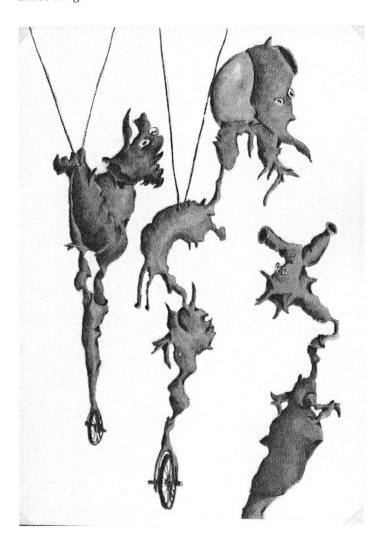

do dive
dull duck
do doze
dork deal

door dirge
chip cheer
dusk dew
duke duel

dab dash
chin chink
dim dark
dog dawn

dank dive
deep debt
dour dose
deam dead

ding dong
dug dirt
ditch dib
chimp chore

damp dank
death do
deed deal
duck dell

do deem
dawn down
dark deep
dog dawn

dig ditch
deed done
dead duke
ding dong

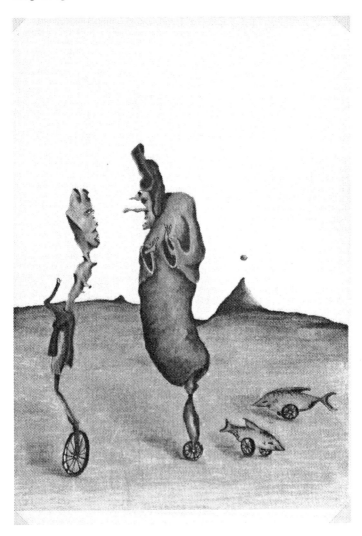

IV. Heliopolis

Suddenly, Last Summer
for Rod Smith

Sun worshipper I, in the absence of the sun, in the
things I don't remember, the unfriendliness of night,
the neon night and blue blue night, the creatures
on the beach,

Suddenly, to remember the sun and all the creatures
on the beach, suddenly to remember the sun and
little sunstroked turtles, suddenly the neon night
surrounding little turtles all surrounded by the night
upon the turtles on the beach,

Sea creatures and mergansers, the blue blue night,
the turtles on the beach all worshipping Apollo, suddenly
I am thrown into your library, never to be what I was
before, surrounded by a tiny light inside the dark and
clutching little turtles,

Go back upon the beach and remember the sun,
suddenly, surrounded by neon, go back, go back to the
beach and worship it, go back to what I was before,
a worshipper upon the beach, Apollo's, in the lavender,
beside mergansers at the sea's night shore.

O Life Force of Supernalness of World

O life force of supernalness of
world, o supernalness, decapitated
mice upon the tracks, o ear muff
head gear of the subway trains in
spring, o the day I saw Lou Reed
on a sidestreet near 6th Avenue, o
jubilance of paper cuts and paper
clips and snow, the small dot on
the page above the snow, the
telephone, the radio, the snow, o
spring, o snow, the snow, the sno
cones and the ski lifts of the snow,
the snow, terrific snow it is, the
spring, the snow, the lack of snow,
the snow itself, o snow, yourself,
the snow upon the human engine
as it waits to be the snow, go out
and be the snow, unloved and
melting in reflections in the grass,
illuminated on the beds of god, you
snow, the crescent jerk of snow, the
city of snow and the city of bacon
and the city of the snow, the
permission of the snow to be the
snow, its lack in spring unlike the
bacon, jerks of god, and snow.

Ye White Antarctic Birds

Ye white antarctic birds of upper 57th street,
you gallery of white antarctic birds, you
street with white antarctic birds and
cabs and white antarctic birds you street,
ye and you the street and birds I walk upon
the galleries of streets and birds and longings,
you the birds antarctic of the conversations
and the bank machines, you the atm of
longing, the longing for the atm machines,
you the lover of the banks and me and birds
and others too and cabs, and you the cabs
and you the subtle longing birds and me,
and you the conversations yet antarctic, and
soup and teeming white antarctic birds and
you the books and phones and atms the bank
machines antarctic, and you the banks and
cabs, and him the one I love, and those who
love me not, and all antarctic longings, and
all the birds and cabs and also on the street
antarctic of this longing.

Poem Beginning with a Line by Frank Lima

And how terrific it is to write a radio poem
and how terrific it is to stand on the roof and
watch the stars go by and how terrific it is to be
misled inside a hallway, and how terrific it is
to be the hallway as it stands inside the house,
and how terrific it is, shaped like a telephone,
to be filled with scotch and stand out on the street,
and how terrific it is to see the stars inside the radios
and cows, and how terrific the cows are, crossing
at night, in their unjaundiced way and moving
through the moonlight, and how terrific the night is,
purveyor of the bells and distant planets, and how
terrific it is to write this poem as I sleep, to sleep
in distant planets in my mind and cross at night the
cows in hallways riding stars to radios at night, and
how terrific night you are, across the bridges, into
tunnels, into bars, and how terrific it is that you are
this too, the fields of planetary pull, terrific, living
on the Hudson, inside the months of spring, an
underwater crossing for the cows in dreams, terrific,
like the radios, the songs, the poem and the stars.

O Razorback Clams
for Daniel Kane

Because it is sad, the people
in the menus in the restaurants
in the bar, because they are sad,
the menus and the windows
and the restaurants and the street,
because it is sad, the restaurant
and the windows and the menus
that they're in, because they are sad,
being hungry and then also being
sad, being listening to the news,
being here beside the windows, and
the airplane, and the sky, because
it is this, sad, everywhere, in the
windows with the windows in the
windows in the stores, with the
windows near the ovens near the
stores beside the street, with the
ovens near the windows near the
tiny bales of hay, because it is
Sunday, and I am sad, and the
windows they are sad like bales
of hay, because the telephone is
sad that calls the restaurant with
the food and there is food and it is
sad, because of the giant sadness
of the food, with bales of hay, beside
the barn, that is a restaurant, where
my sadness is, and this, the food,
the long lines of the couples and
themselves, forkless and sad,
wrapped in plastic, behind the glass,
like sad and lonely lobsters as they
wave inside the oceans in the breeze.

Moo Is Om Backwards

That the cows moo in the field, that the cows moo in the field quite loudly, that the cows are mooing in the field, that in the field the cows are mooing, that I love things, that they love me back, that the cows all love each other and the daisies, that the daisies love each other and the cows, that by loving in transcendence there are cows and there are daisies that they love, that in loving cows and loving cows and loving there are daisies, that the daisies sing but not the cows, that the singing daisies sing, that the singing daisies sing their songs to cows and then the cows do moo, that the mooing cows in fields moo to the singing sounds of daisies, that the mooing and the singing cows are mooing at the sound of singing daisies, that the mooing and the singing in my dreams must cease, that the cows must sleep and love the daisies singing, that the sleeping daisies mooing love the cows, at night, asleep, in mooing at the daisies in the field.

Song of the Chinchilla

You chinchilla in the marketplace in france
you international chinchilla, chinchilla of the
plains and mountains all in fur you fur of the
chinchilla of the pont neuf, selling wrist
watches, on the oldest bridge of evolution that
you are, you, chinchilla, going roadside towards
the cars, the dark arabian chinchilla of the
neutral zone with pears, you still life of
chinchilla, abstractions of chinchilla, aperitif
chinchilla, lowing in the headlands in my mind,
dark, the cliffs of dover, dark chinchilla, tractor
of chinchilla, chili of chinchilla, chill of the
chinchilla, crosswalk of chinchilla of the dawn,
facilitator you, chinchilla, foodstuffs for the
food chain dressed in light.

You, Armadillo

You, armadillo, the dark and stately shape of armadillo,
the street the shape of armadillo, the arm of armadillo in
the cask of snow, the cask of snow in armadillo in the taxi
in the snow, the taxi cab of armadillo, the shape of texas
like an armadillo, the snow that falls in texas in the
armadillo snow, the armadillo running through the street
to zoos in arm's length near the snow, the there you are
where I am not an armadillo that does not light the way,
who likes to draw the armadillo in the foothills of the
stars, the stars of armadillo flesh on grills and acrobats
who eat them, the eaten armadillos and the circus freaks
and jerks of stars, the casks of snow on stars in flames, the
bus boy armadillo, the snow storm armadillo, exploding
armadillo in the tent of night where stars are poles of
armadillos lacking fur and walking through the galleries
like pansies in the rain, the simple bird of armadillo, the
armadillo armadillo in the blades of grass that drift inside
the armadillo dressed like stars inside the blades of night.

On the Lemur

That they loved to go on unmistaken, that they loved
to not to be gratuitous or cry, that they loved the
fortitude of yaks, that suddenly they loved the whiskey
and the sunlight and the key, that they loved the corn
cow and the cow corn that it ate, that they loved the cat
food as it rolled across the floor, that they liked and
loved the coffee that was warm inside the day, that
they loved the sound of hail and what it broke, that
they knew they loved the river that was made where
people dream, that they loved the loins of lions and of
lambs, that they loved confusion and the tools, that they
loved the whistle of the evening train, that they loved
the drugs they dreamt they loved and took inside the
dreams, that they loved their pictures taken and the
sides of barns, that they loved all outer space.

Aardvark

Aardvark with the monkeys in your hair,
aardvark that languishes on the edges of the margins where the
    margin walker walks,
aardvark that you are the sky,
sunken chested aardvark of the dark earth of the aardvark
    gone asleep,
aardvark of the bloody teeth that fall from bloody trees,
aardvark of the sea spray that is green,
of the sea light in the afternoon with rain,
aardvark towards the aardvark running towards the aardvark
    towards the gun,
gunshot wounds of aardvarks and of pepsi cans and teeth,
aardvark of the carnivals,
aardvark of the carnivores,
aardvark of the simple minded men with big head on the plains,
great duende of the aardvark,
lesser duende of the aardvark,
aardvark of the wood grouse that is the aardvark of the loon,
abraham lincoln of the aardvark,
totem animal that is the aardvark wrapped inside the aardvark
    in alarm clocks late at night,
aardvark of the summer of t.v. inside the basement of the
    twilight of the past,
aardvark that eats men,
aardvark that is parent to the cow,
aardvark made of thigh bones built in angles cooked with bells,
aardvark,
factually deflected,
beside the bigger of the trees,
aardvark of the quick and also aardvark of the dead,
aardvark that falls outside of airplanes towards the icy sky
    at night,
screaming aardvark,
head bent to the wind,
aardvark of the sky turned upside down,

maker of the starlings that the aardvark tends to be,
vociferous drunken aardvark that is cast out into time,
beneath the coral,
made of pearls,
aardvark of the aardvarks of the aardvark who is flawed,
aardvark made of milk and cooked in tamarind with lambs,
aardvark redolent of rain,
aardvark redolent of thunder,
aardvark redolent of lizards and the claws of things and men,
aardvark running into spirals toward the ships,
ship aardvarks,
numinous,
unleashed like dogs beside the sea,
of birds as auguries of what the aardvark comes to be,
of the red grain of the wheat fields near the bluish aardvark sky,
of the corn rows of the love of aardvark that is like unto the love
        beside the lamb,
of the hotel rooms of aardvarks that are filled with aardvarks
        arching as to fly,
aardvarks that abound,
contracted,
containing heat,
the candle in the aardvark with its axis on its head,
aardvark in the place where aardvarks breed,
reptiliant,
massive,
brooding,
circular,
shooting widely through the sky at night,
the burning rocks of aardvarks that connect to aardvarks that
        connect up to the rain,
the train ride of the aardvark that is where the aardvark is,
assured, awake, and like an aardvark not shaped like a ball,
the aardvark in a sphere of light,
finally, harmonious,

without disgust,
disguised not as the donuts nor the cockroaches nor planes,
this, aardvark,
single simple aardvark dressed in light,
untouched by what the aardvark is,
with artichokes,
electrical,
arcing as the turkey does
with power in its wings,
of the aardvark in its faithfulness,
overbitten,
exaggerated,
with the element of sun beams
that the elements of aardvark
in its glory yet will be,
break light of the aardvark
in its dance
that in its dance
the numened aardvark brings.

Song from the Greek

for Bill Luoma

On the shoulders   of the tracks
       is where

     the sea green   bends the train
       and tunnels
          run to trains

    with sleek dogs
       on the tracks,   training,

           so spake he,
           Achilles,
           and he sat he

     and the trains did bend   with ships
     and ships bent   by the shore

       and bending brilliant dogs ran
       like the trains   on tracks
       with minds   like dogs

          on sea green days
        with mindful sea green shades
           of dog songs

in the wooden ships   of trains

    that bending,
    sleek,

     toward dogs,

  then spake,
    in trains,

with thoughts of green,

the brilliant dogs of thought,   thinking like the gods,

totally together,
in unison

like trains:

these thoughts of the sea,
this green of the dogs,   shiny

on their tracks

beside their hollow doors.

Lake of Fire

I will make you understand, I, being who I am will
make you understand who I am, on a Sunday,
in the rain, when the ice is melting on the stoop,
beside the white water lily, having been made
to understand that I will make you understand,
making you this, the one who understands, having
understood, standing by it, in the rain, understanding
where I stand I stand near you, the stoop, in the rain,
by the lily, who I am, making sense, understandable,
and smart, and also lovely, that you understand
that it is this, lovely, the truth, in understanding,
having said it, having been understood, like the
rest of the universe, stoop-like, egyptian, with a
lake of fire and the lilies and the train, beautiful,
happy, gleeful, joyed, and understood, this, I am,
who am to you who understands.

The Song Between
after Philip Lamantia

Break your bird on your beak, bird, with a title known as bird,
with a bird sound called a bird, with a bird, being birdlike,
being all bird, in the shallow water, being all water, in the
shallow bird, being the shallow sound of the bird spray in the
wing, being the wing of the sound, bird, being where you are,
being all, and the water is the shallow of the sound inside
the bird, a shadow in the window of the man;

where is the bird that is the stop watch in the street, where is
the sky that is the bird sound that is sound, where is the
shallow where I dreamed about myself, up, between the clouds,
and balanced on the clothesline, where the stop watch stops
the clouds, and all the clouds, shallow, filling up the sky and
from the window where the man did walk, that the man
did walk from the window, that the man did walk, near a
mourning dove, so attentive to the line,

look, up at the clouds there is not one bird and is not one heart,
but is the sound of the clouds which is the sound of a mourning
dove, which is where the window is, steep and near the beach,
where the bird turned, swimming,

and while it is still this, it is morning, and there is no
stop watch, but I think there is a bird, and here in the
shallows of its breast is me, inside a dream, beside
the line that hooks me in, hooked, into the
midtown rain, bird, the hawk that takes the buildings
where it is, you, library of birds, covering the land mass,
miles and miles of all the bird where the sun comes up,
and it shines against the window, and the bird rises
above it, in song, beside its train.

Old

As in the old days
for the wolves who speak
because themselves are
old, in trees, silent,
in the trees above the
heads of silent wolves,
the old and silent wolves
in trees who there are
quiet in the trees that
are so old themselves,
the wolves who eating
soup from cans are old,
the cans of soup that
are as old as wolves,
and I am old this year,
older than the trees or
all the wolves, in their
houses with the heaters
and the stoves and t.v.s
and the cans of soup,
and this is my old song,
that the wolves sing
from the trees, that
the wolves have sung
in dreams.

The Eightfold Path

The human animal that I am
is the human animal that I am

the view that I have is of
the human animal that I am

in the human room,
where I am humanly lonely

and the human moth exists
against the human lamp

and the right view falls in love
with the wrong view,

and the clock of the human city
with the human cars and the noise

from the parking lot, human,
reappears and blinks

to the human confusion
in its naturalness, tired,

I am, the human one,
near the side of the road,

on an escalator, in a human mall
and still the heart goes on

in the human chest against
another chest of earth in human love,

loving the human, fortunate,
in all that is alive.

RIGHT ASPIRATION

This form that misses
its mother, this form
that spends the day in
bed, this form, the more
adorned it is, with much
whispering, with finer
forms of thrills, the form
of the ground that rises
from the Etruscan ruins,
the form of the people
of Pompeii, this form in
the name of the rivers
and the wind, and
the months and its days,
this form, the cover of the
countries dressed in black,
this form of forms of towns,
the forms of trees, of islands,
and the heat, this form of
heat that falls from the
sky, this form of sky,
like a sledge hammer
falling from the heat,
happy again, the form
that hears the form above,
of form from overhead.

Right Speech

Love, which is meaning
compels speech, speech
which is human, compels
mammals, from the trees
of the language of the
mammals, from the mailbox
where they rise, speakers,
hugged close to the
forest fires late at night,
tigers, cicadas, and trees,
name of the one who is love
compels speech which is
meaning from trees to be
mammals, mammalian,
made of music, made of
tigers with the flames,
rising up from the gardens
of the naming of the night,
giant, speaking to me,
content with this, the trees
with tigers and with corn,
the hot spell of speaking
speech, the language laced
with tigers laced with night.

Right Action

O Eros, mangier than I, the nervous coils
about the window with a magpie
in the garbage bins at night,

O form of who I love, trembling thumbs
in need of their own suffering,
the shy gruesome facts of all the matter

in fine poverty chinawear with fire
fine as fair, unfair and not fair, fairly
full, the full moonlight of this

abounding, breaking into parts, together,
under the glow of a simple lamp, who he is,
poor and always hungry filled with flame.

RIGHT ENERGY

To the right of the mind
of the mammal that is
in the dark with the light
from the sea, musical,
in the rain, beneath the
tigers in the lamplight
with the flame, having
feelings of the feelings
that there are, alight,
arrayed in light, arrayed
in what is light inside
itself, so spake it, this
array of autumn in the
trees, the curve of the
branch of the ship
that I love as I love of
its songs in its longing.

Right Mind

Very discrete the moon rises at night
like I do with the bats, where I am
a body and there are other bodies
and let me show them where they are
beneath the bats beneath the moon
in bed beside the bird inside a tree
beneath the cat beside a branch
that is a bed where is the spectre
of a snake dancing, and the body
unfolded unfolds beneath the moon,
spectral, undisturbed and sweet
while the moon pulls, back to the mind,
bears up in the sky, the clouds, single
stars, the life here, of the moon
that is mindful and creates all that is
discrete, unfrivolous, and loved, this form
untouched and shouldered by the night.

Right Labor

What does not change
is the will to change
the humans on the train,
to know more humans
than one has to
who are the humans
on the trains
that go unchanged,
and changing,
as the humans do,
on platforms of the stars,
with windows which are
windows of the starlight
of the trains, with windows
of the humans which are
windows of the night,
bereft of coffee, bereft
of windows, bereft
beneath the stars,
the changed and lovely
humans that are
humans on the trains,
arranged, awaiting
for the will to change
to make arrange
the will they have
to change.

Right Meditation

What thoughts I have tonight of you,
myself, with the razors in the bathroom
on the shelf beside the drugs inside the
rain, and the neighbors who are quiet
inside August in the courtyard in the place
where I have lived, with the cat upon the
windowsill who watches at the moon,
with the moon where it should be, near
the fifth floor there and up into the sky,
in the drift that is the color of the snow
across the surface of a lake inside my
head, talked to and speaking in return,
in this dream, obvious, in prophecy, with
life beyond the passage of the night.

The Specific Incendiaries of Springtime

Inside of my inspection house there are
things I am inside of lacking only linens
and the tiniest of birds, there are small ideas
of tiny birds and things they are inside of,
in the middle of the small ideas of genius
we began inside of sundown,

I am hiding from relationships of springtime
in the tiny rooms with tiny birds, and there
are functions of relations, there are springtimes,
there are tiny birds and checkbooks and some
farmteams,

I am wanting only lemons where you have
wanted only linens in the center of the room,
I am waking up in long corroded rooms,
near Bakersfield and farmteams, in the vivid
dreams of rain, having dominion over these
animals and the salesmen on an island in
relationships with shepherd girls who carry
soft umbrellas,

Toward sundown, let me say that I am in
your absence forced to read a smallish book,
to read ideas of farmteams in the twilight
in the spring, where on an uninhabited
island I strangled all the shepherd girls and
then became a smallish book, and doused
the bed with kerosene he sleeps in doused
with birds and twilight books I dreamt of in
relations of the springtime that I dream,

Of farmteams, clearly let me say of sheep
and clearly let me say of spring in Bakersfield,
where I have strangled all the sheep and
several shepherds, where to read ideas
of twilight in a book, today, to a new love,
where in briefly retouched currency, functions
of inspections in the house now lacking lemons,
here I strangled all the shepherd girls and birds,

Where I read ideas of twilight to a newer love,
where the genius of liberty we began in the
middle toward sundown was a smallish bird
in spring outside of Bakersfield, where,
on an uninhabited island, to the twilight
of this genius in the book, to the mouthpiece of
the smallest sunlit bird, of the farmteam in
corroded blue relations, of ideas and in
inspection blocks, of occurring in the middle
of the twilight, of the dreams of smallest books
and salesmen inside Bakersfield, of wanting
only linens having wanted only wicker in
the center of the room,

I am a soldier of this wicker chair, I am
brandishing a welding torch and drill,
I am the island with the shepherds and the
sheep, I am waking up in Bakersfield in
rain, in a long corroded room, near the
farmteams in the vivid dreams of rain,
and in turning in the kerosene being slowly
doused in fire, I am, toward sunlight,
strangled by a shepherd girl, I am a salesman
of the islands of this currency,

Of rain, let the farmteams in relations
with the springtime in the checkbooks
find the rain, corroded I am, wanting only
lemons, only linens and then you, let me say
that you are on an island with umbrellas,
that we are woken in a room of springtime
birds, that nowhere is a smallish book,
and in the twilight reach dominions of our liberty.

Printed in the United Kingdom
by Lightning Source UK Ltd.
110328UKS00001B/28